Technology Transformed
How Jesus Would Navigate the Digital World

Table of Contents

Chapter 1. Introduction

Explore a unique fusion of spirituality and technology with our special report: "Technology Transformed: How Jesus Would Navigate the Digital World". Unravel the mystery of marrying timeless Christian philosophy with modern technology in a refreshing narrative that takes you beyond the conventional discourse. This thought-provoking exploration hypothesizes the choices and decisions Jesus may make in an era dominated by tech giants, algorithms, and AI. Far from a solemn brow-furrowing study, our report adopts a cheerful and engaging tone, translating profound reflections into everyday language. It's a veritable feast for curious minds ready to explore fresh perspectives! Grab this intriguing journey through faith and pixels which will not only light up your intellectual circuits but also invigorate your spiritual core. Sign up today and let the digital genesis begin!

Chapter 2. Setting the Stage: Ancient Morality Meets Modern Tech

From the sands of an ancient Middle East to the silicon chips of the contemporary world, the bridge of ethics is continuously being constructed and reshaped. In the profound light of Christian philosophy, characterized by the teachings of Jesus, the dialogue between morality and technology uncovers intriguing vistas and challenging conundrums.

2.1. Jesus, the Stone Age, and the Emergence of Morality

Let's first take a spiritual journey back in time. In the days when Jesus wandered the hills and towns of the Middle East, technologies, as we understand them today, were primitive at best. From the chisel to the plow, each tool required human hands to operate. The idea of technology had not yet supplanted the human's central role in the production and management of resources.

The seeds of morality were planted and nurtured in these times. Steeped in the belief that every human is created in the image of God, Jesus propagated a morality of compassion, empathy, and love. The Sermon on the Mount underscores these teachings. These ethical codes, from loving one's neighbor to turning the other cheek, represented a conscious interaction with one's environment.

2.2. Modern Technology: A Quantum Leap

Fast forward to our era, where smartphones are ubiquitous, virtual reality blurs the bounds of perception, and AI-driven algorithms influence our actions. The digitization of processes has displaced human hands from many tasks once considered intricate and personal. This transformation is profound—it represents more than progress; it signifies a paradigm shift in our reliance on and negotiation with technology.

How can a morality tailored for human-to-human interaction cope within this sea change? The disparity seems overwhelming until we consider that the human spirit, regardless of the external context, remains the bedrock of all actions.

2.3. The Analog-Digital Convergence

Let's cut to the quick. Although the worlds of Jesus and modern technology are poles apart, they are not mutually exclusive. The teachings of Jesus remain relevant, not because of their preservation in holy scripts, but because they navigate the complexities of the human heart. Beneath the surface of pixel and silicon, it's this pulse of humanity that technology serves.

Whether we're connecting with friends over social media platforms, using GPS-enabled apps to traverse unfamiliar terrains, or employing AI to predict and prepare for future trends, fundamentally, we're engaging with one another and the environment. And this engagement is where Christian philosophy extends the olive branch to technology.

2.4. An Ethical Matrix: Christian Morality and Tech Responsibility

The digital leap doesn't necessitate a complete overhaul of our moral codes. Instead, it allows for their remodeling and extension. If technology is at our service, then the onus falls on us, the users, to ensure that this power is used responsibly.

In the corporate world, this responsibility translates into producing and implementing technologies guided by ethical principles. Similarly, as consumers, we bear the obligation to utilize these technologies conscientiously. Borrowing from Jesus' philosophy, this translates into empathy, care, and respect for self and others, irrespective of the digital divide.

2.5. The Age of Paradox: Digital Empowerment vs. Digital Dystopia

As we move through the Digital Age, the paradoxes are accentuated. On one hand, technological innovations provide us with unprecedented power and accessibility; on the other, they expose us to the realities of cyber-crimes, digital espionage, and privacy breaches. Such dualities compel us to integrate our ethical beliefs with digital wisdom.

Drawing upon Christian morality, our plunge into the digital deep needs careful discernment. As fascinating as the future painted by technology seems, it's a landscape we must traverse with a compass wired to our moral core. Here, Jesus' teachings serve as not only foundational pillars but also as navigational aids to ensure one does not stray in the dazzling labyrinth of lights.

The balance our ancestors maintained between each other and their tools begot a harmonious relationship that, in essence, is not different from the relationship we might cultivate with our advanced digital interfaces today. The interface has become more sophisticated, the user more nuanced, but the essence of interaction and moral responsibility remains unaltered.

In the synergy of ancient Christian principles and modern technology, we find an incredible opportunity for growth and comprehension. Navigating this digital world, like Jesus might, isn't about mastering code or algorithm but rather about translating timeless messages of empathy, compassion, kindness, and love into our pixels and processes. This marriage of principles is the cornerstone of a world where care and compassion pulse through the screens, animating the stark body of technology with the illuminating spirit of morality.

Chapter 3. Exploring Jesus' Ethical Stances Through a Digital Lens

In the visage of the Son of God, we see an embodiment of love, compassion, and righteousness. But how would these enduring principles translate into a digital context? Let's venture into this thought experiment together, bearing in mind that the interpretations presented are largely speculative, designed to provoke reflection rather than to prescribe exact ethical pathways.

3.1. The Sermon on the Mount: Reimagined

Would the Sermon on the Mount, arguably one of the most influential speeches in recorded history, been tweeted? Or perhaps broadcast on a live Facebook feed? If so, how would Jesus likely have engaged with the ensuing conversations? Quite possibly with kindness and consideration for each individual comment, regardless of sentiment. He may have found a way to ensure the conversation was uplifting and enlightened, delicately moderating the space to prevent it from degenerating into contentious or demeaning dialogue.

In our personal social media interactions, this can serve as a reminder of the power and influence we possess as individuals. A single comment, tweet, or share can create a ripple effect in the vast digital ocean, either contributing to a more enlightened, compassionate society or provoking discord and misunderstanding. As we navigate these digital spaces, let us cherish and maintain the civility and respect that Jesus demonstrated in his interactions.

3.2. Privacy, Transparency, and Trust

In this digital era marked by significant privacy concerns and the often clandestine collection of personal data, how would Jesus approach these complex issues? Given his teachings on truthfulness and respect for individual dignity, it's plausible to argue that he would champion transparency and privacy rights.

He, too, might find himself frustrated with hidden algorithms that exploit vulnerabilities or control the flow of information. Frequently, the encroachment upon personal privacy happens without our explicit knowledge — cookies track our web activity, social media platforms analyze our preferences, and AI technology makes predictions about our behaviors. From Jesus' perspective, this might represent an ethical grey zone — manipulating human action without explicit consent.

Although transparency is an ideal worth striving for, Jesus might also respect the fact that complete transparency is neither possible nor desirable in the digital world. Some level of opacity is crucial to protecting individual rights, nurturing creativity, and fostering trust among digital actors.

3.3. Love Your Online Neighbor

The golden rule that Jesus shared with us in Matthew 7:12, "So in everything, do to others what you would have them do to you...", can also apply powerfully to our digital interactions. In a digital age, this might imply adequate credit for online creators, forbearance in the face of offensive comments, and practical assistance for less tech-savvy individuals.

This principle might also extend to a discourse on digital division, advocating digital inclusion where no one is sidelined based on their digital competency. A move to recognize this inherent digital divide and bridge the emerging gap may indeed align with Jesus's intentions.

3.4. Reconciliation and Restoration in Cyberspace

Cyberbullying, online harassment, and trolling – wreaking havoc in the virtual world – are stark realities of the digital age. In navigating these troublesome waters, the Jesus we know, with an elemental message of forgiveness and reconciliation, might advocate for a path of communication and understanding, over and above immediate punitive action.

A potential consequence of this standpoint could be the emergence of digital safe spaces and fostering of a restorative rather than punitive internet culture — a swing from cancel culture to conversation culture.

This interpretation does not condone negligence or leniency towards online offenders. Restorative justice incorporates accountability and change from the offender's end. On a broader scale, this would underscore the ethos of empathy, compassion, and discourse in our digital interactions.

3.5. Wealth in the Digital Era

The Bible often mentions how difficult it is for those who are rich to enter the kingdom of heaven. In a digital context, this might pertain to the concentration of power and wealth with Big Tech companies. Can this wealth and power concentration be ethical? The likelihood is that Jesus might prod these companies towards the betterment of society, through generous giving and more equitable business practices.

3.6. Stewardship of Technology

Lastly, as Christians are called to be stewards of God's creation, how does this translate when the 'creation' is a complex web of technologies and digital devices, networks and algorithms? While our dominion over devices and data may seem abstract compared to tending physical landscapes, there are numerous ways in which we can live out these stewardship principles - through promoting sustainable tech practices, advocating for ethical usage, and ensuring the benefits of technological advancements reach all sections of society.

Seamlessly blending Christian philosophy and the digital world is certainly a challenging path, but one brimming with countless opportunities for heightened understanding and appreciation of both. Jesus would likely offer a radical perspective on our current digital reality, posing questions that challenge us to reconsider our practices, and pushing us to rethink our digital ethics in the light of his teachings. As co-creators of this digital world, let's heed the call to infuse it with values of love, respect, and justice that Jesus so profoundly embodied.

Chapter 4. Decoding the Digital Age: Insights from the Sermon on the Mount

In the spirit of intellectual exploration and spiritual investigation, let us turn our attention to the Sermon on the Mount, a cornerstone of Christian faith, and explore how its lessons might apply in the digital age. To light our way through this thought-provoking journey, we will utilize forward-thinking perspectives, contemporary analogies, and asciidoc syntax for clarity.

4.1. The Beatitudes in Bytes and Pixels

"Blessed are the poor in spirit...Blessed are the meek." The Beatitudes, a collection of divine blessings and moral teachings, opens the Sermon on the Mount. Now, imagine translating these quintessential principles of humility, mercy, and peace into the realm of technology. Suppose we reframed "poor in spirit" as acknowledging our limitations in the face of constant technological advancement? Indeed, to be "meek" in the technology world is to perpetually appreciate the renewable assets of learning and empathy. This calls for humility in acknowledging one's lack of knowledge, openness to learning, and prioritizing ethical considerations over personal ambition in innovation and development.

Digital proponents and users alike often bow to speed, novelty, and cutting-edge design. Yet, the Beatitudes call us to infuse humility and moral consideration into every digital pursuit. Rather than rejoicing in having the latest, fastest, or most 'disruptive' technology, we should also celebrate those who use technology to foster unity, fairness, and inherent respect for all humans.

4.2. The Art of Digital Peacemaking

"Blessed are the peacemakers...." Today's online environment is rife with discord, hate speech, cyberbullying, and misinformation. Navigating such a world, the teaching of being a peacemaker takes a fresh, profound dimension. In the digital landscape, peacemakers are those who consciously strive to foster online etiquette, challenge divisive narratives, promote respectful dialogue, and combat the spread of fake news. They work actively to create digital experiences that champion peace, understanding, and love over discord and division.

4.3. Salt, Light, and Data Protection

"You are the salt of the earth... you are the light of the world." Consider how this metaphor can apply to the world of cybersecurity. As custodians of data and information, we need to counteract digital corruption (be the "salt") and illuminate areas obscured by ignorance or manipulation (be the "light"). This involves helping to prevent data breaches, respecting privacy norms, creating transparency in data usage, and empowering users with knowledge about how their data is managed and used.

4.4. Love Thy Digital Neighbors

The foundational Christian principle of "Love thy neighbor" gains fresh relevance in the digital realm where a 'neighbor' can be in a physically distant location but virtually next door. Online interactions provide unique opportunities for both fellowship and spreading positive digital footprints, where anonymity can often incite to malevolence.

Embracing the digital application of this principle means exercising respect and kindness online, protecting others' digital rights, standing against cyberbullying, and celebrating diversity in the global digital neighborhood.

4.5. Seek, Ask, Knock, and Search Engines

"Ask, and it will be given to you; seek, and you will find; knock, and the door will be opened to you." The faith-filled promises Jesus shares here effortlessly align with our digital search behaviors. With a click or a voice command, we set forth a petition (search), seek, and find. But in the age of algorithmic bias and bubbles, we must remain discerning searchers, alert to the implications of the answers we receive, and eager to continue our exploration beyond predictive analysis.

To deliberate and reflect upon one's search, or to knock on the less-explored door, are efforts against the passive consumption of technology. Just as Jesus urged proactive seeking and knocking, he would perhaps prompt us to question the algorithmically-directed reality, urging for conscious navigation, enriching the digital exploration.

In closing, the Sermon on the Mount, even when applied to the digital world, serves as a guideline to foster an ethical ethos online and to utilize technology responsibly and respectfully. Its timeless wisdom, far from scoffing at our technological ubiquity, or becoming obsolete technology, can help us harness its powers holistically. Thus, it lights up our intellectual understanding and invigorates our spiritual core to strive for a digital world echoing the spirit of humility, love, peace, and righteousness- a heritage Jesus championed in his Sermon on the Mount.

Chapter 5. Walking Through Silicon Valley in Jesus' Sandals

The glimmering lights of Silicon Valley, a metaphor for the technological advancements it represents, come into focus as we begin our unique journey. Clad in ancient, well-worn sandals, let's try to comprehend these advancements through the lens of traditional Christian philosophy.

5.1. A Vision of Human Enhancement

The concept of human enhancement through technology might seem alien in the context of 1st-century Judean understanding, yet it's a reality we find ourselves negotiating daily. The idea of devices that extend our human capabilities, like Google's vast information repository or SpaceX's ventures into space travel, would surely astonish even the insightful Jesus.

However, we hypothesize that Jesus would not reject these tech marvels out of hand. Instead, he may interpret these as mankind's God-given ability to learn, explore, and innovate to survive, and even thrive. At a foundational level, there would be a recognition of technology as an extension of human creativity, innately good because it is rooted in the image of the Creator.

5.2. The Shadow Side of Human Innovation

Yet, every coin possesses two sides, and we need to confront the shadow side of our technological utopia. From data breaches to the misuse of social media, the list of potential misuse is alarmingly long. And when we consider Jesus's emphasis on purity of the heart and love for one another, it's essential to scrutinize the ethical concerns involving privacy, data security, and the good of the community.

We can safely assume that Jesus would approach the issue with wisdom and discernment. He would not demonize technology but would instead call us to greater responsibility. Highlighting the dignity of every human being, he may propose stringent data privacy laws or online standards mirroring the virtues of honesty, integrity, and respect taught in scripture.

5.3. Technology and the Neighbor

A common thread that runs through Jesus's teachings is the commitment to the health and well-being of our neighbors. Silicon Valley is a melting pot of various cultures and economic classes. Unfortunately, the rapid march of technology often leaves disadvantaged communities handicapped.

Given Jesus's concern for the marginalized, it is safe to presume that he would press for initiatives bridging the digital divide. These could include affordable tech education for all, equal access to broadband services, and efforts to spread digital literacy among the disadvantaged.

5.4. Technology and Leisure

Silicon Valley signifies a culture of workaholism, where burnout is often worn as a badge of honor. Yet, remember Jesus's emphasis on the Sabbath, a day of rest and reflection. In a world governed by 24/7 availability brought about by smartphones and laptops, Jesus's perspective offers a refreshing emphasis on rest and restoration.

Jesus might urge tech companies to institute policies promoting work-life balance. The necessity of downtime for creativity and health would, we believe, be strongly emphasized, reevaluating our relationship with technology as a tool, not as a taskmaster.

5.5. Entrusting The Future

Through the blinding lights of Silicon Valley, in Jesus's sandals, we gain a uniquely hopeful vision of technology's future. It calls us to balance the scales of liberty and responsibility, power and restraint, innovation and tradition, in ways that do not compromise our spiritual foundations.

The journey through Silicon Valley might seem overwhelming. Yet, armed with the insights from the life and teachings of Jesus, we can navigate these digital pathways with newfound wisdom and awareness. After all, Jesus's philosophy was always about discerning the way, the truth, and the life. And this journey through the modern Tech Valley reaffirms that it's the way we use technology that defines our relationship to it, and more crucially to each other, noting that the goal is not to abolish technology, but to humanize it.

Bearing this in mind, we can stride confidently into the digital future, our sandals leaving imprints in the Silicon sands of time.

Chapter 6. Proverbs in Programming: A New Kind of Beatitudes

In the time-span of few decades, programming languages have become the firmament of our digital world, just as Proverbs were, and continue to be, a beacon of wisdom for Christian believers. As we traverse this unique intersection of code and Christ, we'll explore a new kind of beatitudes, inspired by classic teachings yet tuned to the dynamics of a digitally-driven culture.

6.1. Writing Syntax and Living Righteously

In a way, following a programming style guide can be akin to following a moral code. Programmers adhere to strict syntax rules, keeping their code clean and understandable. Similarly, living righteously demands adherence to a strict moral syntax where our actions reflect our faith.

""Blessed are the geeks; for they shall inherit the Internet" is a playful twist on Matthew 5:5. Coders, with their knack for solving complex problems and building intricate systems, can pave the way for an ethical, inclusive digital realm. It serves as a reminder that the God-given privilege of intellect comes with a responsibility to use it for good.

6.2. Functions of Faith And Code

Functions encapsulate complex operations and simplify the process of execution, much like how prayer simplifies our communication with the Divine. They both serve as conduits between complex realities. Emulating Proverbs 3:5, we could redesign it for the code era as, "In all your algorithms, acknowledge Him, and He will make your paths bug-free."

This principle teaches us that no matter how intricate our code, or how tangled our logic may seem, assuring that our actions fall within a moral and ethical framework (highlighting fairness, inclusivity, privacy, etc.), we can create technology that is both effective and beneficial for all users.

6.3. Loops of Life and Algorithms

While loops in programming bring automation and efficiency to repetitive tasks, our lives often enter loops that seem monotonous. The modified Psalm 23:1-4 could read, "Even though I walk through the darkest valleys of code, I will fear no bugs, for you debug with me; your IDE and your function, they comfort me."

This expresses the faith that in the tedious trials and debugging sessions, we are not alone. It's not just about solving problems in isolation, but about recognizing that these difficulties mould us into better programmers and individuals.

6.4. Conditional Statements and Free Will

Just as conditional statements control the execution of code based on certain conditions, free will allows us to choose between right and wrong, thus controlling the execution of our life. A programmer has the responsibility to account for all potential conditions to ensure their code runs smoothly. Similarly, we, as humans, have a moral obligation to consider our choices, and their impacts, thoroughly. The Leviticus 19:18 in code lingo might read, "If thine enemy errs in his code, correct him: you must love your neighbor as your own code."

Understanding the implications of our actions and always choosing the path of compassion and empathy aligns us with moral righteousness. That's a nod to how constructive criticism and collaboration, even in the face of conflicting viewpoints, can uphold the ethics of programming.

6.5. Comments and Reflection

Just as comments in code help programmers navigate through complex logic, prayer and meditation help Christians navigate their spiritual journey. A moment of quiet reflection can untangle knotted thoughts, much the same way proper commenting can smooth out the coding process. "Think before you commit code, for it will be your offering unto the software" puts Acts 20:35 into a programming context, reflecting how diligent work paves the way for more fruitful programming.

Taking the time to reflect on our intentions and actions, both in programming and life, leads to robust outcomes. It fosters a sense of fulfillment rooted in the quality of our actions, not merely their end results.

6.6. Conclusion

In conclusion, the fusion of Proverbs and programming serves as guideposts for those navigating the symbiosis of faith and technology. Infusing our code with the essence of timeless wisdom helps not only in creating more efficient and effective technology, but also in creating a more compassionate and thoughtful technology culture. As we learn to navigate the convergence of these two worlds, the new kind of beatitudes that emerge can light our way in creating technology that is helpful, humane, and harmonizes with our morality.

Programming and Proverbs are not dichotomous; each paradigm teems with wisdom to enhance the other. By synthesizing these perspectives, we can foster a technology culture that cherishes wisdom as much as wit, compassion as much as code, and ethics as much as efficiency. With this transformed understanding, believers and programmers alike can co-create a cognitively diverse, inclusive and human-centric digital world.

Chapter 7. Building Cyber Bridges: Universal Love in the Digital Age

In the digital realm, where emotions and sentiments are transformed into emoticons and reaction emojis, how do we amplify the resonances of universal love Jesus propagated? Let us embark on this journey to demystify the complex interweavings of spiritual bindings and binary codes.

One must begin by considering the words of Jesus, 'Love your neighbor as yourself'. Twisted by digital waters, this runs deeper than familiar definitions of neighborly love. In the online expanse, the geography of our neighborhood has changed; it is not defined by physical boundaries but in terms of our interconnectedness.

7.1. Unpacking Universal Love in Digital Times

In the gospel of Luke, Jesus narrates the parable of the good Samaritan, a tale that beautifully transcends tribal, racial, and social boundaries in the pursuit of love and kindness. If we read this tale with a digital lens, everyone connected online, irrespective of geographical, cultural, or racial difference fits under the umbrella term 'neighbor'.

Historically, our neighbors have been those in our proximity, with communication limited by physical distances and upheld by similarities in culture and dialect. Now, the internet has thrown open the doors to global neighbors. This imposes a conscientious reckoning of our actions, not restricted to the physical world alone, but in the digital airspace we frequent.

Jesus' teachings helped to establish the central role of love in our lives. The challenge before us now is to reinterpret these age-old teachings in an age dominated by hashtags and handles. Can technology assist us in this mission? Can tweets and posts carry the heavy load of universal love?

7.2. Digital Morality: Evolving Ethical Frameworks Online

In Paul's letter to the Corinthians, 'love is patient, love is kind. It does not envy, it does not boast, it is not proud', we find a call to elevate our online conduct. Daily, we are privy to negative news, hate speech, cyberbullying, and a myriad of damaging digital phenomena. Undoing such habitual patterns requires an updated take on Paul's letter.

In applying this to our updated moral framework, we borrow the universality of Jesus' teachings and add a dash of innovation. Online love needs to be patient, even in the onslaught of differing thoughts. It should be kind towards a varied spectrum of perspectives and ideas. It should not envy another's online success or popularity. In a realm that so readily showcases our achievements and milestones, it should not boast or inflate egos. Above all, it should promote humility, and not pride.

7.3. Techno-Altruism: Using Digital Platforms for Good

The era of social media platforms and the internet is rich with opportunities to exercise and spread universal love. One might argue we are on fertile ground for techno-altruism, where we bring the love of Jesus to action digitally.

Consider the abundance of crowdfunding platforms. They serve as lifelines for those in need, irrespective of geographical location. Money can be raised for a vast array of purposes - unexpected medical emergencies, education funds for disadvantaged youth, or resources for relief efforts in disaster-stricken areas. The force behind these platforms? Universal love in action, a neighborly extension to the extreme.

It's important to balance this optimism with a certain degree of caution. The misuse of digital platforms can generate harm, spreading hate and promoting division. It's here that the teachings of Jesus become not just a moral compass, but also a guideline for empathetic digital footprints.

7.4. Conclusion: Wiring Love into our Digital DNA

Concluding our exploration of universal love in the digital age, we find ourselves faced with an array of challenges and opportunities. It's clear that the teachings of Jesus, when applied thoughtfully, can guide us towards healthier, more positive digital interactions.

Key to our conversations about love, be it offline or digitally, are values of patience, kindness, humility, and respect. The digital universe opens up vast opportunities for expressing these values. Jesus' commandment to 'love thy neighbor' rings true today with more urgency than ever, urging us to inject love into our digital DNA.

The narrative of universal love remains unchanged despite the shift in our communication mediums over centuries. And it's our test to carry forward that narrative in the digital era successfully, according to the teachings of Jesus. Technology will keep evolving. Our challenge and opportunity lie in ensuring that our underlying principles follow suit, protecting the essence of universal love.

Chapter 8. Miracles 2.0: Compassion in the Time of AI

We start our discourse with the gentle reminder of Jesus' miracles that brought about profound alterations in people's lives. Here, we aim to showcase an elevated understanding of compassionate acts in our present world that seems to be dominated by artificial intelligence.

8.1. The Modern Nazareth: AI in Today's World

In the grand tapestry of technological evolution, Artificial Intelligence (AI) stands out much like the biblical city of Nazareth in the Gospel's narratives. A city renowned for its ordinary splendor, Nazareth was also the setting for extraordinary miracles and transformative teachings by Jesus. Similarly, AI, with utility in ordinary tasks, also possesses the power to manifest extraordinary changes in the world.

Though AI lacks a beating heart or the capacity to imitate human emotions, it does have the adaptability of a curious mind. It gains wisdom from patterns, predicting probable outcomes, and adapting accordingly. Likewise, AI lacks any spiritual identity, yet it is governed by a sort of codified set of instructions, not unlike the life guidelines provided to all Christians.

8.2. Parables of Benevolence: AI in Healthcare

If Jesus were to interpret modern miracles, the compassionate application of AI in healthcare may certainly be counted. When AI collaborates with medical expertise, the result resuscitates hopes of new life, much like Jesus raised Lazarus from the dead.

With pattern recognition, medical imaging analysis, drug development, and prediction of disease onset, AI systems can illuminate paths to healing otherwise unseen. AI expands healthcare's capabilities, improving diagnostics, patient treatment, care, and even managing pandemic situations effectively.

While it's crucial to understand AI's utility, we must be aware of its limitations too. AI can't replace human doctors or answer the patient's emotional needs, spirituality, and faith in their healing journey.

8.3. The Good Samaritan's Code: AI in Social Work

Another vital area where AI acts as a modern 'Good Samaritan' is its deployment within social work. Employing sentiment analysis, identifying deep fake content, monitoring human rights abuses, or even managing refugee crises - AI plays a significant role.

AI algorithms act on behalf of those unable to voice their concerns - mirroring Jesus' teachings to stand up for the silenced and oppressed. However, AI has limitations. We must govern these creations cautiously, maintaining transparency and accountability.

8.4. Simon's Cyberspace: AI in Education

In the era of remote learning, technology has become a steadfast ally to many. AI offers educational opportunities to unprivileged areas, reminiscent of Simon of Cyrene aiding Jesus carry his cross. Customized learning, teacher support, and increased accessibility are some of the benefits AI offers.

While technology can bridge gaps, it also risks widening the digital divide due to disparities in resources. This calls for thoughtful implementation, ensuring that the gifts of AI are equally shared.

8.5. The Last Supper's Bytes: AI and Ethics

Perhaps the most crucial area where AI aligns with Jesus' compassionate teachings is ethical programming. AI systems can be developed to prioritize empathy, equity, and environmental sustainability. However, as AI holds no inherent values, ethical codes must be conscientiously programmed by human engineers.

This raises questions of control, influence, and misappropriation of technology wrapped in the guise of 'how it contributes to the common good.' It calls for discernment to ensure that behind every miracle of technology, the bedrock of compassion, justice, and love remains - principles that Jesus cherished dearly.

As we ponder the evolving role of AI, it's essential to maintain a delicate balance. Miracles 2.0 encompass benefits for all, displaying a compassionate spirit synonymous with Jesus' teachings. In this age of AI, faith communities must engage in a dialogue with technologists to foster ethical, spiritual, and humane technology that still upholds the tenets of compassion, love, and justice central to Christianity.

Chapter 9. Casting the First Cyber-Stone: Faceless Judgement in the Age of Social Media

The advent of social media has redefined our approach towards communication, essentially transforming us into both consumers and creators of content. On these platforms, individuals find a voice, an outlet for expression, and in our contemporary society, these voices often harmonize into choruses of praise or rebuke. Such dialogues have given rise, regrettably, to an echo chamber, a cycle of anonymous judgment echoing through the depths of the internet. This virtual world of judgment presents an intriguing premise: how might Jesus have navigated this landscape saturated with virtual stones?

9.1. The Spirit of Anonymity

Our journey into the heart of digital judgment begins with understanding the phantom of anonymity. Anonymity on social media is a double-edged sword. On one hand, it provides a mask of safety, granting everyone the courage and freedom to express ideas without the fear of reprisal. However, the same cloak of anonymity can heighten tendencies toward unwarranted harshness and snap judgments.

In this context, let's reflect on John 8:7, "Let him who is without sin among you be the first to throw a stone at her." In the digital world, anonymity acts like the veil of sinlessness, inviting users to cast virtual stones impulsively. Jesus might have appealed to the humanity behind each digital identity, nudging them gently towards compassion rather than condemnation.

9.2. Soundless Voices, Impactful Echoes

While our social media engagements may seem momentary and fleeting, their echoes linger far longer in cyber-universe. Each hasty, misplaced judgment or thoughtless comment can ricochet through the digital space, causing psychological harm. Bearing in mind Jesus' teachings about loving one's neighbor, he might have reminded us that our virtual neighbours deserve the same respect, kindness and understanding.

9.3. Compassion Amidst the Impersonal

Social media platforms, while fostering connection, can also paradoxically foster a certain level of impersonality fuelled by anonymity. However, if we were to reenvision these platforms through the lens of Christian thinking, they could be seen as avenues for promoting empathy and compassion. Jesus, known for touching the lives of marginalized individuals, might have made a case for leveraging social media to amplify the voices of the unheard, the neglected, and the misunderstood.

9.4. Guardian of Our Digital Eden

The virtual world, much like the Garden of Eden, is a place of vast potentiality, ripe for both the sowing of constructive dialogues and the spreading of malicious judgments. As children of Adam and Eve, all too familiar with the consumption of the forbidden fruit, we seem to be impulsive in passing judgments, forgetting the teachings of our spiritual mentor, Jesus.

9.5. Navigating Through the Digital Sea of Galilee

Jesus calmed the stormy Sea of Galilee, and similarly, he might have suggested practices to calm the stormy seas of our digital world. This could involve promoting digital literacy, fostering spaces for constructive dialogues, and advocating for forgiveness for digital missteps. On the tempestuous seas of social media, invoking principles of understanding, and encouraging patience in the face of confusion or difference, Jesus might have been a beacon of peace.

9.6. The Virtual Good Samaritan

Online platforms provide an opportunity to become a 'virtual Good Samaritan'. They offer countless opportunities for users to help each other, promote positive content and foster a community of empathy and understanding. Undoubtedly, Jesus would have advocated for the rise of more such Samaritans, emphasizing the power of compassion in our digital interactions.

In essence, our digital actions matter, given their potential for both harm and healing. If we were to hypothesize Jesus' digital behavior, it would undoubtedly be one marked by kindness, compassion, and understanding. As we navigate our way through this digital age, let us aspire to adopt these virtues in our online interactions, refraining from casting the first cyber-stone in haste. Through this, we cultivate a more positive, empathetic digital landscape, echoing the teachings of Jesus himself.

Chapter 10. Ethical Dilemmas at Data's Last Supper

As the clock of civilization relentlessly ticks forward, we find ourselves seated not around tables of wood, but tables of data, where bits and bytes replace the bread and wine of yesteryears. The ethical conundrums served at this updated Last Supper are multitudinous and complex, where unseen digital hands grapple with dilemmas that would startle even the learned Pharisees.

10.1. The Algorithm Inquisition

The modern technocrat worships at the altar of algorithms. Revered as tools of efficiency and progress, these mathematical constructs weave their invisible webs around our lives, dictating our routines, preferences, and even emotions. But do these god-like algorithms merit their hallowed status? Would Jesus approve their judgment?

Jesus, a figure of empathy and compassion, valued the uniqueness of each soul. This sentiment diametrically contradicts the algorithmic penchant for pigeonholing people into convenient categories and labels, thereby reducing complex human realities into narrow datasets. Furthermore, algorithms are designed by humans, carrying an inherent risk of subjective biases. The case of biased facial recognition technology stands testament to these prejudices played out on a global scale.

If Jesus walked among us today, he might question the role of these algorithms in our life. He might argue that while they can help us manage our time, tasks, or find like-minded communities, they should never supplant our freedom to make independent, informed decisions.

10.2. The Ghost in the Machine

In the hypothetical gospel according to Silicon Valley, artificial intelligence emerges as a charismatic protagonist, capable of miracles rivaling those of yesteryears. As the curtain lifts on AI's capabilities, we witness the blind seeing through bionic eyes, the deaf hearing with cochlear implants, and even the lame walking through robotic limbs - miracles touted upon the digital stage.

Yet, with extraordinary capabilities come extraordinary moral implications. When AI takes over fields like healthcare, finance, or judiciary, it holds sway over life and death, wealth and poverty, guilt and innocence. In such instances, machines fail to replicate the wisdom, moral compass, or compassion of Jesus. They become Brutus, wielding the proverbial knife with no regards to consequences.

Presumably, Jesus would like us to utilize the fruits of AI to alleviate human suffering. However, he might caution us about the irresponsible use of AI, reminding us that it is a tool, not a deity, and should always be guided by human values and ethical integrity.

10.3. The Social Media Messiah

Social media has become the pulpit of the digital age, its reach unparalleled in human history. The positive influence of social media is undeniable, from the Arab Spring to the Black Lives Matter movement. Yet, this megaphone of modernity has a dark side.

Defined by echo chambers, spiteful comments, and disinformation, social media challenges our understanding of truth and reality. As Jesus noted, "the truth will set you free," but can this freedom be attained when truth is shrouded by manipulative algorithms and malevolent actors?

If Jesus were among us, he would surely advocate for the responsible use of social media. He might champion the potential of such platforms for uplifting messages, fostering community, and promoting justice. At the same time, he might remind us not to lose ourselves in the digital cacophony, urging continual introspection and grounding in our shared values.

10.4. The Virtue in Virtual Reality

Similar to how Jesus used parables to convey his teachings, we find parallels in virtual reality offering immersive, compelling narratives. The ethically tangled web arises when we question the realism of these experiences.

The conundrum lies in distinguishing right from wrong in a fabricated reality. Actions committed in the virtual world might not have real-world consequences, yet they shape our character and morality. Would the Sermon on the Mount hold any meaning in a realm where consequences are an illusion?

Jesus might warn us that while the allure of escaping to a virtual Eden may be strong, we must remember that our decisions, even in digital spaces, echo in our conscience, and we are accountable for our actions, both to our own selves and to our community.

10.5. Conclusion

In conclusion, the ethical feast at this digital Last Supper provokes us to reflect, question, and debate. Technology's luminal glow illuminates the pathway to progress but casts long shadows of ethical dilemma in its wake. Just as Jesus urged discernment and righteousness in his disciples at the Last Supper, we are called upon to keep these virtues at the heart of technological development.

Remember, these technologies are merely tools. Crucial to realize is the truth that we, humans, are their makers, guided by the moral compass received through millennia of wisdom including Jesus's teachings. When entangled in ethical dilemmas, let's recall those teachings, for they are our beacon through the digital maelstrom.

Chapter 11. Resurrecting Humanity: Leveraging Technology for Greater Good

In the beginning were the Word and the verse, the idea and the expression. These elements were fundamental in spreading the teachings of Jesus. The same principles of communication are critical today as we stand wedged between the analog past and the digital future, navigating our way through the era of technology with the wisdom of Christ.

11.1. The Gospel in the Digital Age

Imagine Jesus walking among us in the digital age. Picture him sharing parables over Twitter, healing the blind with biotechnology, or promoting the teachings of love and forgiveness through an interactive app. If the purpose of technology is to make our lives better, augment our abilities, and connect us to one another, wouldn't the perfect symbiosis be to use technology for the Greater Good?

In Christianity, the term 'resurrection' denotes the act of rising from the dead. In the context of this chapter, 'Resurrecting Humanity' implies a revival of the essence of humanity by leveraging technology. Here, we seek to identify the choices Jesus might make when employing modern tech tools to perpetuate his eternal teachings of love, peace, and compassion.

The internet has popularized many otherwise hidden viewpoints, illuminating dark corners and exposing truths. The explosion of information shared online has served as both boon and bane, furthering enlightenment on the one hand and spreading misinformation on the other. The conundrum here isn't the technology itself, but rather how we use it. If Jesus were among us today, what might be his approach to these powerful yet double-edged tools?

11.2. The Ethical Dilemmas of Technology: A Biblical Perspective

Despite its many wonders, technology has a darker side, from privacy breaches to harmful misinformation and online hatred. Yet, the Bible guides us in understanding this ubiquitous entity. In 1 Corinthians 6:12, Paul writes: "All things are lawful for me, but not all things are helpful". This principle applies perfectly to our technological world. While there are myriad opportunities to employ tech tools, not every use promotes good or exhibits Christ-like behavior.

For instance, social media platforms offer powerful ways to connect and share messages. They also harbor the potential for harm, fostering polarized echo chambers and facilitating fake news. If Jesus were on Facebook, his actions likely wouldn't merely revolve around accumulating followers but using the platform to foster genuine, caring communities.

The same thinking could apply to Jesus's handling of privacy and data ethics. The Bible and technology may seem worlds apart, but the timeless principles of honesty, respect, and care for others find new applications in today's digital age. Jesus might advocate for ethical data practices that respect individual privacy, potentially using technology to guide individuals towards responsible and informed consent.

11.3. Reverberating Christian Love through Artificial Intelligence

What about Artificial Intelligence (AI)? Humanity's newest technological frontier has spurred conversations both exciting and disconcerting. If Jesus were to engage with AI, what stance might he take?

AI, in its current form, is a reflection of its creators. It learns from humans, mirroring both our strengths and flaws. It can echo God's love or spew hatred, spread truth, or disseminate deception, depending on how it's steered.

AI applications such as recommendation engines can foster beneficial communities, learning user tastes to make helpful suggestions. If Jesus were leveraging this tech, he might encourage a design that amplifies positive conversations, promotes growth, and aids in making users more empathetic, more compassionate, more Christ-like. Moreover, Jesus might push AI farther, promoting its use in medical diagnostics, humanitarian aid, and education, unleashing its potential as a force for good on a global scale.

11.4. Building Bridges, Not Walls, with Blockchain

Finally, an examination of the potential synergies between Jesus and technology would be incomplete without considering blockchain. Beyond simply supporting cryptocurrencies like Bitcoin, blockchain's promise lies in its decentralization and transparency, concepts echoed in Jesus's message of equality and truth.

Blockchain can empower marginalized communities, giving identity to the undocumented or financial access to the unbanked. Jesus might advocate blockchain solutions as tools to manifest fairness, integrity, equality, and love - the pillars of His teachings.

In conclusion, Jesus, were he to navigate today's digital world, would likely not reject technology. Instead, he might utilize it to extend his role as a healer, teacher, and savior. He could harness social media, data, AI, and blockchain for the greater good, epitomizing the resurrection of humanity in a world increasingly shaped by technology.

Technology and spirituality can co-exist and even thrive. An understanding of Christian philosophy helps us navigate ethical dilemmas in the digital world. When we leverage technology with the wisdom and compassion of Jesus, we create a powerful tool that can genuinely serve humanity.

In the end, the seamless fusion of spirituality with technology might herald a new era, resurrecting the very humanity we fear losing in the information age and the dogged pursuit of cutting-edge tech. In Jesus's hands, these tools for connectivity and information could shape a world closer to the principles imparted in his teachings, offering a potent reminder that in a digital world, the human element matters the most.